Smelly
Old History
Victorian Vapours

Mary Dobson

OXFORD UNIVERSITY PRESS

Oxford University Press, Great Clarendon Street, Oxford OX2 6DP

Oxford New York Athens Auckland Bangkok Bogotá Bombay
Buenos Aires Calcutta Cape Town Dar es Salaam Delhi Florence
Hong Kong Istanbul Karachi Kuala Lumpur Madras Madrid
Melbourne Mexico City Nairobi Paris Singapore Taipei Tokyo
Toronto

and associated companies in
Berlin Ibadan

Oxford is a trade mark of Oxford University Press

© Mary Dobson 1997
First Published 1997
1 3 5 7 9 10 8 6 4 2

Artwork: Vince Reid and Mark Robertson. Photographs: Image Select/Ann Ronan Picture
Library: 15; The Mansell Collection Ltd: 11; Science & Society Picture Library: 25 both.

A CIP catalogue record for this book is
available from the British Library

ISBN 0-19-910095-0

Printed in Great Britain

CONTENTS

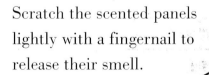

Scratch the scented panels
lightly with a fingernail to
release their smell.

A SENSE OF THE PAST

A boy chimney sweep

Can you imagine what it was really like living in Victorian Britain? It was certainly smelly. The streets were littered with horse dung (and much worse), the poorest families crowded into stinking slums with no running water, even the rich and the Royals had no protection against foul and fatal disease.

Of all the senses of the past, we often forget the importance of smell! This book takes you as close as possible to smelly old history. It's filled with the smells of our past for you to scratch and sniff – the horrible and the heavenly (but mostly the horrible).

Queen Victoria came to the throne in 1837, and reigned for nearly 64 years until she died in 1901. Many Victorians believed that the foul vapours of their towns, countryside, homes, drains and bodies were the cause of disease. They did not see the germs lurking in the mud. They did try to improve their smelly environment. They drenched themselves with perfumed vapours to disguise the disgusting stench, and they invented some very clever new stink traps.

Selling violets on the street

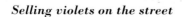

4

Victorian Vapours

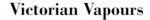

Nightsoil men empty the toilets

Victorians really tried their best
To throw out all their stinking mess.
Too bad it landed on the street,
The dung, the muck, the rotting meat.
They stank their streams with smelly rot
From sewers, pits and chamber pot.

The factories belched out lots of smoke
With noxious vapours full of coke.
They turned us black, they turned us pale.
Tho' laws were passed, 'twas no avail.
The sun went out, the dark fogs hung
With poisonous fumes that hurt the lung.

The ladies faint with vapours fell,
And perfumed salts they had to smell.
In London there was worse to come –
The Great Stink showed what they had done.
The Thames with rot had filled and filled,
Till cholera came and thousands killed.

Crossing sweepers

The doctors went to sniff the slaughter,
They missed the bugs but smelt the water.
From that day on they tried to clean
Their sewers, wells and every stream.
They bought a flush from Mr Crap,
And thus enjoyed a new stink trap.

The rich began to smell quite nice,
They washed their clothes and lost their lice.
The poor were sadly left to stew,
They weren't even offered a decent loo.
How could the Victorians be so mean
To leave us with this smelly scene?

HEAVENLY SCENTS

Life in the country could be rich and rosy, with rural smells of fresh grass, fragrant flowers - and pig manure! The Victorian family living in this house in the country is quite well off. They have six servants, including a cook. From the kitchen come delicious aromas of baking bread, herbs, fresh vegetables and roasting meat on the range. And the garden's full of roses. *Scratch and sniff the roses opposite, and let their heavenly scent waft you back to this idyllic Victorian scene.*

But before you get too
carried away with these
fragrant reminders, consider these
pungent facts:

🌹 The flowers, fruits and plants grew so well because
of all the stinky dung and sewage that was brought from
the cities and dumped as fertilizer on the fields and
gardens. (Perhaps that rose doesn't smell so lovely after all.)

🌹 The expression 'to pluck a rose' meant to go to the privy, or
toilet, in the garden. Privies stank and were full of flies, so the
Victorians grew honeysuckle, roses or lavender around the
door to disguise the foul smells.

7

THE GREAT UNWASHED

Now try and forget those heavenly country aromas. As one of 'the great unwashed' poor growing up in the squalor and filth of a Victorian city slum you would have been surrounded by the most appalling stinks and stenches.

In many of the festering slums, which were known as courts, rookeries or fever nests, there were no proper toilets, no running water and no baths for washing. If you were lucky, water might be available from a pipe in the street for a couple of hours, three times a week (but it probably contained raw sewage). You might have to wade through puddles of stale urine and oozing excrement to reach it.

In 1849 The Times newspaper received this letter: 'Sur...we live in muck and filthe. We aint go no priviz, no dust bins, no drains, no water-splies, and no drain or suer in the hole place...The stenche of a Gully-hole is disgustin. We all of us suffer, and numbers are ill, and if the Cholera comes Lord help us...Preaye Sir com and see us, for we are living like piggs, and it aint faire we should be so ill treted.'

Inside the houses families crowded together in tiny rooms. Imagine sharing your bed with lots of irritating brothers and sisters, as well as itchy vermin and bedbugs. That would certainly have made you scratch and sniff!

One of the worst jobs on the street was as a 'pure-finder' (there was nothing pure about it at all). 'Pure', or decomposing dog dung, was used in making leather, and old men and women gathered it as a final resort rather than go into the workhouse. A bucketful of 'pure' bought a day's lodging and food. Sounds like pure robbery!

Men and children worked in the sewers, catching rats or searching for coins.

THE GREAT STINK

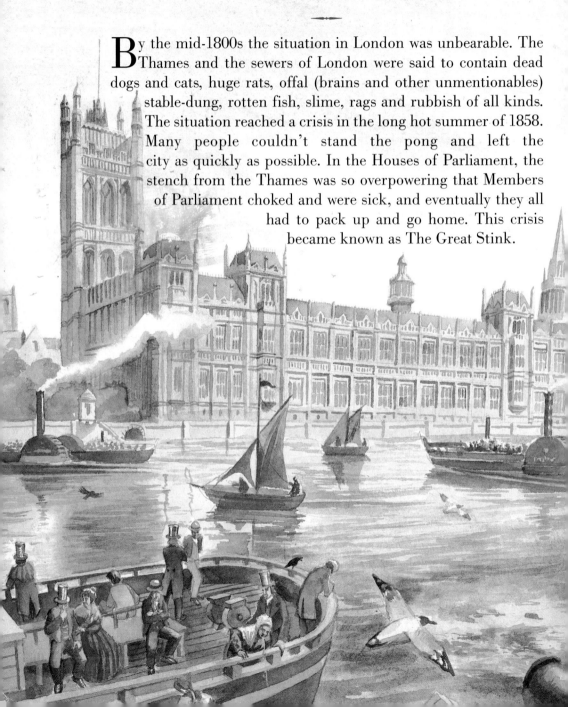

By the mid-1800s the situation in London was unbearable. The Thames and the sewers of London were said to contain dead dogs and cats, huge rats, offal (brains and other unmentionables) stable-dung, rotten fish, slime, rags and rubbish of all kinds. The situation reached a crisis in the long hot summer of 1858. Many people couldn't stand the pong and left the city as quickly as possible. In the Houses of Parliament, the stench from the Thames was so overpowering that Members of Parliament choked and were sick, and eventually they all had to pack up and go home. This crisis became known as The Great Stink.

The Government tried their very best to remove The Great Stink immediately. They sent out a Smelling Expedition to sniff out a solution. Only the sharpest-nosed MPs were allowed to join. They suggested a Stinking Fund, to raise money for a huge drainage system under London. This was such a brilliant idea that one magazine suggested the brave MPs should be given a special award, 'The Order of Nasal Valour' for extraordinary services to Queen and Country.

In this Victorian cartoon the man is giving a message to Father Thames. Can you guess what is floating on the water?

The River Thames became a gigantic open sewer. Imagine the sewage from all over the city pouring into this river. Scratch the panel below, for a truly revolting sense of The Great Stink.

A RIGHT ROYAL MESS

Being rich and royal did not always protect you from the stinks of 19th-century Britain. Queen Victoria and Prince Albert suffered terribly from their odorous surroundings, and poor Albert came to a very smelly end.

 On a relaxing cruise on the Thames in 1858, the Queen faints at the terrible stench. Prince Albert has noticed before that sewage from the overflowing Thames ends up in the gardens of Windsor Castle. Victoria simply orders the royal gardeners to throw it back into the river, but Albert wishes he could do something about the foul water.

 Albert is out admiring designs for new houses for the working classes, which have much better sanitary arrangements. But he's summoned home by the royal ratcatcher and the royal bug destroyer, to deal with a right royal mess at Windsor. The 53 overflowing cesspools are causing a terrible stench, and part of the Castle has had to be closed.

In 1861 poor old Albert, who wanted to improve things, made the fatal mistake of drinking a glass of contaminated water, and catching typhoid – one of the filthiest diseases of the time. The Queen hopes to revive him with fragrant perfumes, but it's all hopeless.

Ten years on, and Victoria's still grieving for Albert. She won't allow any changes at Windsor Castle, not even one of the new loos. Now she's hit with the news that her son, Prince Edward, is close to death with typhoid. Fortunately for his widowed mum, Edward survives (well he has to doesn't he, because he becomes King of England in 1901).

13

ROTTEN REMINDERS

Grave Matters

✠ One in three babies died before their first birthday, in the smelliest parts of Britain. Only one in ten babies died in their first year in the cleanest parts. No wonder bad odours got such a foul press!

✠ If you survived your first year, you could reckon on only another 20 years of life if you lived in a foul-smelling city slum (who could have stood it for longer?).

✠ Before the 1870s, over half the patients admitted to hospital for an operation died. Even when anaesthetics were discovered, which put the patient to sleep, the results could be deadly. One surgeon killed three people in one operation: the patient, the assistant who accidently had his fingers cut off and died from gangrene, and a distinguished spectator who dropped dead from fright.

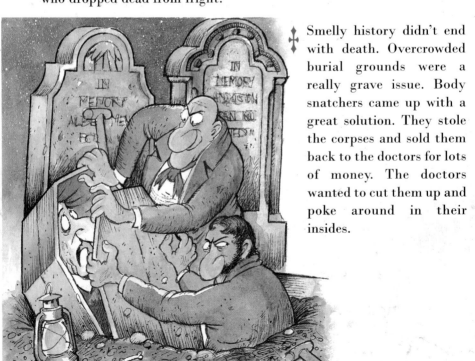

✠ Smelly history didn't end with death. Overcrowded burial grounds were a really grave issue. Body snatchers came up with a great solution. They stole the corpses and sold them back to the doctors for lots of money. The doctors wanted to cut them up and poke around in their insides.

Just imagine the pong!

✠ Every day 1000 tons of horse dung were deposited on the streets of London! Can you imagine what that smelt like?

✠ A public auction was held in one town for the sale of human excrement. Farmers paid high prices for a bit of pungent human manure!

✠ Some foul Victorian stinks were deliberately concocted. Horrible things were added to food to change its appearance or taste. How about milk topped up with sheep's brains, chalk and gum? Or tea made out of sweepings and sawdust?

One contemporary idea for avoiding smells in the street.

✠ In some places, 400 people had to share one or two privies as their toilet. These were holes in the ground with no running water.
Scratch and sniff below to get the full effect.

FOUL AND FATAL

Living in Victorian Britain would certainly have made you sick. There were some terrible diseases about, like cholera, typhus, tuberculosis and smallpox. Many people thought that the horrible stenches around them actually caused these foul and fatal afflictions, and with so much stinking rot and rubbish around, who could blame them!

If you caught cholera, you were in for a really foul time. The contents of your intestines would escape in gushing diarrhoea, you'd be violently sick and probably turn blue. And in your agony no-one would come near you, because you'd smell so awful!

From the 1860s scientists began to discover that it wasn't the bad smells that caused the disease, but germs. But the stinking places and smelly people were the perfect places for these germs to live. The germs and the disease carriers like rats, lice, cockroaches, bugs and fleas were all having a wonderful time in all the muckheaps, sewers and fever nests of Victorian Britain.

The old remedies were still used. Imagine this slimy leech sucking out your poisoned blood!

Victorian hospitals were terrible, filthy places, stinking of death and decay. But gradually improvements were made. Chloroform came in as an anaesthetic in operations, to knock out the patients. Carbolic acid, which kills germs, was introduced for putting on wounds to keep them clean. But some nurses refused to use it – they thought it smelt worse than the putrid wounds!

This poor man is having his rotting leg amputated, with no anaesthetic so he's wide awake. The surgeon used this saw on another patient earlier today, but he has wiped the blood and pus off it, on his apron, before starting. The doctors are wearing their oldest, dirtiest coats – they certainly don't want to make their clean coats dirty here!

SNIFFING OUT THE TRUTH

There were terrible cholera epidemics in Victorian Britain, and no-one saw the germs lurking in the mud. But in 1854, Dr John Snow noticed that all the cholera victims in one district of London had been drinking water from the same pump in Broad Street. He pulled off the pump handle and cholera disappeared from that district. Dr John Snow had sniffed out the truth.

Sam Sewage and his friends live in the sewers under Broad Street in Soho, London, in 1854.

Evil Stinker is the enemy of the underworld. He has the power to mix any stink he wants.

Meanwhile, in the smelly upper world, Dr John Snow, qualified in Recognising Offensive Odours, has found the foulest smell in London.

Down the sewer, Evil Stinker takes aim with his special potion.

Everyone's queuing up for water. Helpless, Sam Sewage is sucked up into the pump.

Forty-eight hours later, Sam and his friends re-enter the underworld.

Death and disease spread through Soho. Evil Stinker is delighted.

But Dr Snow has guessed the cause of cholera. It's in the water!

Evil Stinker watches in horror as Dr John Snow destroys his work by pulling off the pump handle. Sam Sewage and his friends are happy to be left in peace. Determined not to be defeated, Evil Stinker goes to another smelly spot. He knows Dr Snow has sniffed out the truth!

STEAM AND SMUT

Victorian Britain was, without doubt, an extremely smelly and unhealthy place. But there were some exciting new developments and fresh places to visit. This was the glorious great age of steam, with new railway lines across the green, rolling countryside. Now people could travel more quickly than they ever did in the old horse-drawn stage coaches.

Taking a trip to the seaside was one of the most refreshing excursions for rich and poor. At last they could wash off some of that grime.

But there was a high price to pay for the puffing trains – smut! At the end of a long journey in a third class carriage, you might blow your nose on your new white, scented, cotton handkerchief, and after one big snort it would be black.

Never mind, there was really no need to get all steamed up, for the aromas of fresh, salty, sea airs, and rotting seaweed, dead fish, and tons of holiday-makers' rubbish on the beaches of Brighton, Scarborough or Blackpool, would quickly revive your sense of smell.

Beside the seaside

The Viccis they did like the sun,
And sought the sea for all their fun.
It felt so good, it smelt so fresh,
The rotting seaweed was the best.
They dipped, they bathed,
*   they wet their toes,*
But still they had to hold their nose.

TOWN
DRAIN

FACTORY FUMES

As a child of eight working in this cotton factory, you would soon get to know what factory fumes smelt like. Inside the hot, noisy factory you would be sniffing up loads of dusty cotton waste, called fuzz. Inside your crooked little body, you would feel the fuzz winding round your lungs, making you cough, wheeze and spit blood. The factory would be making cotton clothes and linens, but your poor family would never be able to afford to buy them. *Scratch the filthy smoke opposite to get a rotten reminder of factory fumes.*

Out on the street, on your way to work at dawn, or to school after six hours' work in the factory, you would breathe in all the foul fumes from the other factories in town. The worst smells were from the blood-boilers, glue-makers, and the tanneries, which might be using the 'pure' decomposing dog dung that your mother had collected to soften leather hides. The town would be overhung by stinking black fogs, and on a freezing day black snow flakes might settle on your bare little tired arms. But don't try complaining. You would be whipped black and blue by your employer or your school-teacher.

STINK TRAPS

There were stink traps of all shapes and sizes in Victorian Britain. When nature called, you had several options:

- *you could 'pluck a rose' in the garden privy. This was far from private.*

- *you might have a water closet or close stool if you were rich, and even a washbasin too.*

- *you could use a portable urinal or a fancy chamber pot – ideal for emergencies.*

There were also several ways of dealing with the result of your efforts:

- *you could leave it out for the nightsoil men to remove in their lavender tub – but sadly they might only come a few times a year!*

- *you could put it on the doorstep in a bucket, topped up with ashes from the fire, for the middenmen to collect once a week.*

- *you could throw it onto the communal dunghill.*

- *you could let it drain into the local sewers – and see it again two weeks later in your drinking water.*

24

During Victoria's reign several men, for example Thomas Crapper and John Doulton, tried to invent a stink trap that would flush the stuff away. They came up with some very fancy designs for toilets, with names like Niagara Falls, Waterloo, Deluge, Crapper, Rapido and Tornado. Some of these were successful and were used in public. But public toilets cost a penny to use, so only the stinking rich could afford them.

Our modern type of flushing closet, with basin and trap all in one piece, was not available at a reasonable price until the 1890s. Then two qualities of toilets were designed: a castle model for the rich and a cottage model for the poor.

An elaborate chamber pot.

A model of Jenning's flushing water closet, c.1900.

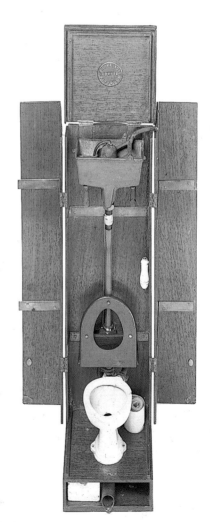

The Victorian Flush

Victorians were so famous for
Inventions, gadgets, tools and more.
But did you know that pride of place
Is owing to their smallest space?
They sought out ways, they looked for means
To channel off our basic streams.
When first they chanced upon the flush
Victorian ladies turned to blush.
But then it caught on good and clean,
To 'spend a penny' soon was seen
A perfect way to pass one's lot,
Far better than the chamber pot.
That humble little flushing pot
Deserves more fame than it has got.
What would you do without your loo?
(Any clean answer here will do.)

THE SWEET SMELL OF SUCCESS

However hard and smelly life was for the poor, Victorian factories were churning out thousands of amazing products. In the summer of 1851 a Great Exhibition of inventions and goods was held in Hyde Park, London, in a huge glass and iron building called the Crystal Palace. Britain had become the industrial centre of the world, and the Great Exhibition was a powerful reminder of the sweet smell of success. Six million people visited it. One woman, aged 85, walked all the way from Cornwall!

The latest Victorian invention.
The first paying public toilet
was at the Great Exhibition.

The Great Exhibition was overflowing with fresh, new products – there were 727 exhibitors in the soap and perfumery section alone. There were deodorants, disinfectants, soaps, perfume bottles, scented lamps and many other fragrant and exotic temptations, to cover up even the most revolting domestic stinks. And of course their makers became filthy rich.

Perfume bottles

Baths of all shapes and sizes became more popular.

Chocolate bars were invented in 1847 and on show at the Great Exhibition.

Scratch and sniff for a sweet smell of success.

27

FRAGRANT REFRESHERS

Victorian ladies often had 'the vapours'. This meant they fainted. Some blamed their tight corsets, but others said it was because of all the vile Victorian vapours. Ladies were revived with 'smelling salts' like vinegar, lavender or scent.

The Victorian 'vapours'

Flowery-smelling perfumes, especially roses and lavender, were very popular as fragrant refreshers. In early Victorian times, most people hardly ever had a bath, so sloshing on these strong scents was a great way of covering up their Victorian body odours.

The perfume industry flourished under Queen Victoria. A person who tested perfumes was called a 'nose'. At the Great Exhibition in 1851, over 270 gallons of perfume were distributed to visitors.

A 'nose'

The Victorian Christmas could be deliciously smelly, with sugar and spice and all things nice! In Dickens's story *A Christmas Carol*, Tiny Tim and the Cratchit family savour the wonderful smells of roast goose, sage and onions, crackling chestnuts and rich Christmas pud.

A merry, smelly Christmas

The Victorians thought it would be a good idea to make all children go to school, but it cost the same to spend a day at school as to use a public lavatory. (Where would you rather spend a penny?)

To everybody's relief, toilet paper was finally invented in the 1860s.

By the end of Victoria's reign, life for many people was less smelly. They were healthier and lived longer. Doctors knew that germs caused disease, and that they thrived wherever it was dirty and smelly, so they encouraged people to keep clean.

Sadly, not everyone could afford a bath. For many poor people in the industrial cities, life was still filled with more rotten reminders than fragrant refreshers.

The public baths

BLESS THIS HOUSE

PUNGENT PUZZLES

🌸 There is at least one smelly word for each letter of the alphabet. Have a go at creating your own alphabet of Victorian smell words. (eg. A is for aromatic, B is for beastly, C is for cholera, D is for disgusting...X is for xtremely smelly, Z is for zoos.)

🌸 These are all names for the same smelly place:

boghouse, *comfort station*, **gong house**, houses of parliament, *monkey closet*, SHOOTING GALLERY, reading room, **halting station**, *the necessary house*, **the you know where**, *latrine*, PLACE OF EASEMENT, ***temple of convenience***.
Guess where?

🌸 Spell the smell:

ktins lesmly

rudoo eeprmuf

oufl ardni

nogp tncse

tpdriu

oulydm

kree

tnnugpe

omraa

twese

rseew

ttnore

kmcu

30

GLOSSARY

anaesthetic	a drug which numbs an area of the body, or puts a patient completely to sleep, before an operation. eg. chloroform.
antiseptic	a liquid used to kill germs on wounds. eg carbolic acid.
cesspool	an underground pit for a privy to drain into.
cholera	a disease caused by germs in water or food.
close stool	a chair or stool with a built-in chamber pot, used as a toilet.
epidemic	a widespread outbreak of a disease.
leech	a blood-sucking worm.
middenman	someone who collected the contents of chamber pots and other refuse from buckets left out in the street.
nightsoil man	someone who collected the contents of privies, usually at night because of the smell.
privy	an outside toilet, with no running water.
pure	decomposing dog excrement, used to soften leather.
slum	an area of very poor housing in a city, also known as a court, rookery or fever nest.
typhoid	a disease caused by germs in water or food.
workhouse	a place for the poor, old and sick who had nowhere else to go. Conditions were terrible and the work was hard.

INDEX